THE SPECTATOR
CARTOON BOOK

Edited by
Michael Heath

P

PROFILE BOOKS

in association with

The Spectator

First published
in book form in Great Britain in 2002 by
Profile Books Ltd
58A Hatton Garden, London EC1N 8LX
in association with
The Spectator
56 Doughty Street, London WC1N 2LL

Typeset by MacGuru
info@macguru.org.uk

Printed and bound in Great Britain by
Bookmarque Ltd, Croydon, Surrey

A CIP catalogue record for this book is available from
the British Library.

ISBN 1 86197 493 0

'I could murder a McDonald!'

*'I tell you what, George —
it's great having your own transport.'*

'That went well, I thought.'

'Who are you staring at?'

'Looks like Joanie lost another gerbil.'

'It was nothing, darling, she's just an old flambé!'

'Excellent! They've found you a donor at last.'

'I've decided to quit acting and writing screenplays in order to concentrate on my waitressing.'

'It's me — I'm on the throne.'

'Who needs a career? I'm proud of being a housewife.'

'And this is his Cynical Period.'

'I've reached the age where I've given up on men
but not boys …'

'Why did we get a cheetah? They need so much walking!'

'Can't we just get a divorce?'

'How did they get in here?'

'It's an extremely reliable source of energy,
and it has no harmful effects on the environment.'

'Here's one of me in France having a hip replacement …
this is me having my cataracts done in Spain …'

'Shut up! That's enough of your "last words".'

'Kevin — it's your "take-away"…'

'OK, those of you going for your brain surgery badge
go and get scrubbed up.'

*'That was a very long and tedious confession.
For your penance you deserve to get a parking ticket!'*

'That was an endangered species!'

'Maybe this wasn't such a good idea.'

'Ah — a fellow non-mingler.'

'I'm not your first one-night stand, am I?'

'A Starbucks will open on your block.'

*'I hear Jenkins caught that bug
that's been going around the office.'*

'How's it going, Joseph?'

'I'm going to shop till I drop …'

'I tried to take it off him, and he bit me!'

'Still heterosexual?'

'Apparently he's well known as the
only non-celebrity in the village.'

'That's funny — it says here that Tuesday is Market Day.'

'Can I call you back? I'm about to go through a tunnel.'

'We haven't had much luck with pets.'

'I was brought up by lesbians.'

'Mm, smells good for a change.'

'The world didn't end. That means I have to start
paying off my credit card …'

'This is one serious health-club!'

'I didn't even know she was angry until she started shooting.'

'I think I'm being followed!'

First Day of School.

'He thinks it's warmer up there.'

'Then we thought to hell with the bridge evening.'

'Oh, for heaven's sake Leonard!'

'Let's see, Miss Jones didn't put anything in
my diary about being abducted.'

'Anything happening yet?'

'Death, War — meet Accountancy.'

'How exciting, Clarissa — he's a *body-builder* and
he's bringing a friend.'

'Are you looking at my bird?'

'Why didn't you mention you were dyslexic earlier then?!'

'Somebody's dropped a testicle.'

'Yeah, the cat's pretty territorial.'

'You're pretty cool for a white guy.'

'You don't like my fancy dress? …
I'm not wearing fancy dress.'

'Leonard, call the pest control people!
This is getting out of hand!'

'Light-brown hair, cuddly, good in bed …'

'This would be a great autobiography if it wasn't for all the stuff about collecting nuts.'

'Welcome to "Cleaning Up". Today we'll be scrubbing the pans that Jacques and Julia used to cook turkey gallantine and duck confit.'

'Why should he be academically inclined? He's not a girl!'

'I've forgotten, Martha — tell me again what it was
you used to see in me.'

*'In your case sex education will form
part of the history syllabus.'*

'Well, it's not my idea of a stretch limo.'

'Me? I held up a train.'

'Well, gotta get up early and start drinking again.'

'We've had complaints about your new cataloguing system, Miss Prebble.'

'That's it, kids — no more hamsters.'

'Hello, coffee tech support?'

'Dog food, dog food, bones. Right, that's it! Tomorrow
you're back to getting the newspaper!'

'Notice how they never ask the real "man in the street"?'

'He bit his first ear off at school today.'

'Can I borrow the leg tonight, Dad?'

'Gosh, isn't your James shooting up?'

brian bagnall

'If you take the last two weeks in Leo,
I'll have a few days in Libra.'

'Perhaps one of these years your Mum
might like to come with us.'

'No — *not* there! There!'

'Thank heaven you're here — they've just about taken over.'